LATE
SUNLIGHT

Poems
by
Judith Burnley

Salamander Street

First published in 2022 by Salamander Street Ltd.
(info@salamanderstreet.com)

Copyright © Judith Burnley, 2022

A CIP catalogue record for this book is available from the British Library.

Typeset in Baskerville by Salamander Street.

ISBN: 9781914228674

10 9 8 7 6 5 4 3 2 1

To my 'Cariad fach'

Contents

Late Sunlight

Glimpses of sunlight in a tree-lined street,
The pavements gleaming after sudden rain,
The beauty of the ordinary world
Sights, smells and sounds of everyday
Tug at the heart now in an unexpected way
And linger.
Do they know
That time is on their side
But we
Have not got long to stay?

A Kitchen Resurrection

It can't be true that you're still dead
When from the ground
As deep as you are buried
New shoots push to light.
Each year their growth, their flowering,
Confound.

I bought a bunch of spring today.
The cost? One pound.
The buds are tight as their green stems
Yet overnight
They'll swell, give birth
And uncurl with the might
Of resurrection –
That great, longed for fable.

Bright daffodils upon a kitchen table.

Kiss

Do you remember one short winter's afternoon
Of fitful sunlight, when
We walked along a deeply rutted lane and came
To the edge of a steep and newly ploughed up field
Curving in ridges open to the sky
And there we kissed. And kissed again.
Young lovers, though we were not young
We longed, just as the newly opened earth
For April rain.

Haunted

I sat down on my mother's bed
And held her hand. She smiled at me.
'She's fading fast,' the carer said.
'It won't be long.'
'Oh, no', I said. 'She smiled when I came in.
She knows it's me.'

'That's how it is,' the carer said.
'That's what they do.
She pulls herself back – for you.'
She left the room.
We were alone.
I knew what I must do.

Her hand in mine was small and dry and warm.
She looks so small, I thought.
How can she be this massive presence in my life?
She lies too still
She who was always busy doing things.
'You can rest now,' I whispered to her,
'You've done everything.
You've loved us and we've loved you.'

Later that night, she died.
Oh, I was full of certainties, back then,
But now I am nearer to her age
I'm haunted.
How had I dared?
Playing God.
Suggesting she let go.
Did I do right?
But I can't ask her
So I'll never know.

Unfurled

I look at my body now with some surprise.
Before I met you, I never knew
What it could do.
Hold, mould, caress, entwine,
Whatever's mine is yours,
Whatever's yours is mine.
All tensions eased, all clenching now uncurled –
Like tender leaves in spring, we lie unfurled.
When you make love to me I know
The meaning of the world.

Tryst

Out of a dark November – rain, pain, near despair,
I sped towards you through a sudden burst of sunshine,
as if
The train knew where you were.

Drenched fields were green-eyed emeralds
And the bare black branches of wet trees
Shed leaves of gold, like coins, into the air.

My key in our secret lock, and the love-nest warm
With aromatic smells, the table laid for two,
And wine and fruit and flowers everywhere.

And there you were, my darling, in a trance
On our old sofa where you'd waited
All night long. You'd had no sleep
Wondering, hoping, doubting we would meet.
Perhaps I simply couldn't get away.
And so you thought I was a vision, 'til
You got your arms around me.
"Oh, you're real," you said.
"Oh, yes. I'm real. I'm here."

Let the world spin on without me
As long as I have this:
The urgency, the longing and the lingering
Of that first kiss.
The slow remembering how our bodies fit.
The Bliss
Of simply being
Us.

Long Pause.

"Come on, it's almost sunset, we're going out.
There's something you should see."
And there, in a pale pink sky
You offered me the moon -
A tiny silver crescent, the rim of a coffee spoon,
So old and wise, but then, to us,
So absolutely new.

Then, from the top of Castle Hill
Trees in the valley darkened, and the lake
Glimmered – a polished silver plate.
Lights lit in distant windows, and evening spread
It's bounty of false promises before us,
Whispering of our future, hinting
At things we never said.

At home, you lit a huge log fire and
Opened the champagne
To toast ourselves, to laugh, to celebrate,
To banish useless rage
That we had found this joy so late
In the twilight of our days.

Perseus' Comets

We're in for shooting stars tonight
We'll see them if the sky is bright
Dripping like diamonds in freefall
From velvets of the deepest blue.

But what do I care if clouds obscure
This Happening from my eager view?
The stars are only meaningful to me
If I am watching them with you.

We should be lying on some grassy slope
Catching the brilliants as they fall
Together.
Alone, without you, I confess,
Such astral high-jinks seem to me
Just weather.

Trees

When I first walked across this room
And saw the trees
Framed in the grace of these high windows
My eyes filled with tears.
Perhaps I sensed I'd live here,
Laugh here, cry here,
More than fifty years.

The trees watch over me
And I watch them
For signs, for portents:
Sunsets when the bare black branches glow,
In moonlight, rain, in cloud or sunlight
And deep snow.

I have grown old here
Though I don't feel old,
But wonder, sometimes, if there'll be another spring.
The trees are stronger, older, bolder
By a century or two.
They'll outlive me,
They won't miss me
When it's time for me to go.

Papa

He always comes back to get me
As I knew he would.
He's strong and handsome, wearing a white suit.
He holds me to him, looks into my eyes:
You must grow up without me
You're a big boy, now.
I'm six years old. I know
I'll never learn to be a man like him.
He turns to go.
I follow him.
The way leads to a tunnel.
It's dark. But I can see his white suit shining.
It has a glow.
Then I wake up. And cry.
I never can believe that I've grown up alone,
Or that he had to die.

The Boy Who Leaned Over Bridges

The boy who leaned over bridges
Saw more, much more
Than treacherous waters, glint of trout,
Or otter's muddy slink.
He learned to spot a kite, or trace a swift,
Follow wild geese in flight, and land
A slippery fish.

He listened to the whirr of insects on the wing,
And felt their essence and their evanescence,
The pulse, the throb, the heartbeat
Of all living things.

So when this boy became a man,
Quick of wit and strong of arm and will,
He leaned over those same bridges
With a secret pounding in his blood,
A secret he wished he didn't know:
Nothing in Nature ever can lie still
Unless you kill.

Paros

This ancient island where the scent of thyme
Can overwhelm the senselessness of Time,
Where wild Aegean winds, the Meltemi, still blow,
And sons of pirates, rich on shipwrecking
Still run the show,
Where cubed white houses in the harbour huddle fast
Against new tempests, surely it was here
That Prospero broke his magic staff at last?

If only I could find it, buried near
In sand dunes, under prickly cedars,
Who knows where?
Some shady corner of these stony streets
Where smell of jasmine and smoke-charcoaled meats
Or calamari fried in olive oil can't spoil
The sea-salt whiff of memories long past –
Those lost aromas.

What I am searching for is just a stick,
The gnarled and twisted branch of some old tree.
I'll find it, mend it, and call back its Power:
Prospero's cunning, the felicity
Of Ariel – I need you, now.
It's desperate, can't you see?
I'm running out of time, but only now
Am learning how to
Be.

Waterloo Bridge

On either side the river lie
The cloud-capped towers, St. Paul's, The Tate,
The wobbly bridge, The Globe, The Shard,
The London Eye,
The secret rooms where men of power
Make and unmake our history by the hour.
And all this bright, pulsating life
Is mine from birth, my own Birth Right.
But soon, one bleak uncalled for night
It will be snatched away from me
And I will never see it more. Oh why
Must I lose all of this, so rightly mine
For some old abstract concept known as Time?
It's a rum deal. Perhaps the Age Police
Will deign to grant me an extended lease?
But no. "Look here, old girl," they'll say,
"You've been here eighty years. We need the space.
Now don't make with the tears."
What if I tell them that my revels are not ended?
Will they relent and say my sentence is suspended?
It's worth a try.
We who inherit London
Are too strong spirited
To die.

Cold Front Moving Over

How did it get to late October, once again?
Last night the clocks went back,
Now its late afternoon and we wait for the rain
To stop raining.
A log on the fire falls, flames spit and hiss.
Are they, too, complaining?

Time and the weather, taken together
Govern our lives.

Man, woman and dog walk, at last, in the woods,
Dog sniffing the trails of badger and fox,
Of rabbits and deer, dead birds – the lot.
We shuffle wet beech leaves, so soft underfoot,
Pretending their brightness will cover the rot.

We're beckoned by bullrushes up a steep hill,
Blithely ignoring
Their tall brown suede heads nodding
Gravely in warning:
They grow in a deep, hidden pond
We could easily fall in.

A hawk searching hawks, you scan the sky.
Buzzards fly up and perch.

Stillness. Then suddenly we see
A world divided
Sharp as new meaning, cut cleanly in two,
Half indigo dark – the cold front moving south –
And half an unlikely clear midsummer blue.

A pale but fierce sun has appeared
And the skyline stands bold:
Those grey, jagged teeth, the old castle towers
Framed by the ruins of venerable oaks.
A lingering glow – old fires not put out,
New stories for old.

We blink and are dazzled, our spirits lift, as if
The cold front has shifted in our souls,
Changing, perhaps forever
Our bleak, internal weather
Leaving us, in harsh light,
Over-exposed.

Time and the weather, taken together
Shorten our lives.
Nature renews itself.
What of us, survives?

Birth Day

What can I send you, darling, on a day
When all your instincts tell you
Hide away?
It will soon pass,
As every year falls faster than cut grass.
All I can do
Is tell you love outlives time's scorn,
And, simply
I'm so glad that you were born.

Instead of Christmas

Standing in your doorway gazing at a frosted half-moon,
Warming your cockles with a dram of old Drambuie,
Watching a white fox from a midnight window
Surprising as a secret, deep in snow.
Searching your familiar woods for mushrooms
Eating them with buttered toast for breakfast,
Driving the hills and valleys of your childhood,
Still and always the boy who leaned over bridges.
Spotting otters, noting a speckled trout or two,
Sighting a white owl flying and a brown owl perching
The same evening.
Know that you move always in my rhythm,
Breathe always to my heart's beat.
Listen.

Grounded

I sit high in my urban eyrie,
Rooftops, windows, and, just breaking into leaf,
The tops of tall plane trees.
But much more clearly, what my mind's eye sees
Are your hands sifting loamy soil
And adding the mature manure
Aerated by fat, glossy worms
You dug from a local farmyard and
Wheelbarrowed to here.

Potatoes will flourish now, lettuces, and runner beans,
Greenhouse tomatoes, so pretty and so sweet
It seems a shame to pick them, let alone to eat.
But run their stamen in your fingers
And they'll waft
The scent of schooldays long forgot.

So while my head is far away and in the clouds
Your feet – and sometimes – hands, are in the earth
Bequeathed to you before your birth,
And knowing that, I'm grounded, too
And sense what our dear lives are really worth.

Big D.

What we're all doing, every single day
Is fighting the Big D
That big black doorway of the mind
That never goes away.
It's always been there, menacing
But we ignore it. Life gets in the way.
We have a cup of tea, a glass of something round,
We have a friend to stay.
We are alive, we make things out of air:
A meal, a song, a marriage, or a table,
But everything we do must prove that we are able
To earn our right to live.
An ageless fable:
The more we love in life, the more
Light years will keep us from that dreaded door.

A Fierce Logic

I wasn't ready to go home, you said, but
There's a fierce logic in the hospital
That when your temperature is steady,
And the drips and wires are all unplugged,
That's it.
They've no more use for you in there.

And so they stand you up and send you off
Helpless as any baby born too soon
Into a cold, uncaring morning light.
No witnesses to see if you'll put up a fight,
Or if you've strength to struggle for
A future not yet in your sight.

I wasn't ready, either, for the shock
Of knowing I could lose you,
So the lock I'd put on fear broke down
Though it was tough.
I'd loved you well, not wisely, for so long,
But clearly, not for long enough.

A Winter Song

The sky was dripping stars last night
But you weren't here.
I leaned against the window pane
And looked for you
But all in vain
In vain.

Snow lay unmelted on the grass
Perhaps this winter will not pass
Unless you're here.

I sat beside the fire last night
The logs were dry, the flames were bright
You were not here.

And yet the fire burned fearlessly
And so I let its' warmth and cheer
Embrace me.
You are always near.

Mother Confronts the Infinite

They put my mother in a space ship, so she said.
They were doing tests.
Lights flashed, white metal whizzed and clicked,
Loud buzzing noises went on off, on off,
Recording parts of her she'd never seen,
Receiving messages she'd never got
From her own inner space.

In all these years of sitting in her favourite old chair
And sipping tea,
This sensible modern woman
Never dreamt
Of inner or outer space,
But only and always, of the here and now.

And yet, today, I wondered, she said, wondering,
Now, when it is too late,
What we are here for, where we are going,

Why we are here at all.

And then, of course, I thought of you, my daughter,
And wondered if you had wondered, too.
And what would become of you, who are here
Because of me,
When I am out there
In that dazzling whiteness that I saw. I mean,
What has it all been for?

How is it possible to live so long
And not know more?

Riverrun

River running clear and fast
To no future, from no past
What almighty hand is here
To conjure water out of air
And keep it flowing down the years
As if all time was made of tears?

River running clear and fast
To no future from no past
Propelled by an eternal force
To carve its everlasting course.
But how the source renews itself
Mere mortals cannot know
Like trees, we're rooted to the bank
And can't go with the flow.

River running swift and clear
A murmur in the inner ear
Rhythmic as breathing
Forceful as leaving
All life's mystery is here.

The Lover

You're in the wrong part, my darling,
Can't you see?
You're meant to be The Prince,
You know the one – rides in on his white charger
Whisks the girl away
From all that kitchen drudgery -
The Lover
It's the best part in the play.

Husbands are lesser mortals
Locked in the everyday.
Their wives are captive creatures
Who never go astray.

That's not her scene at all
She's yearned
For you to rescue her,
She's read the fairy tale.
She won't hang around until
Her daily bread goes stale.

She wants the speed of that white steed,
The open road,
A future quite unplanned
She wants a lifelong lover,
Not a wedding band.

In Touch

All afternoon I watched your hands
Hold, cling and intertwine.
Long fingers interlocking
Silent
As in mime.

No need for words
When touch
Says all you need to know:
I'm here, I'm near,
I'll never let you go.

Corridor

Down the corridor my mother trots
In and out of all her rooms
Gaily, briskly, tired but dutiful,
And never for a moment, still.
She tidies, polishes, arranges every single thing
In her own special way.
There is a rhythm to it: it marks her every day.

But then, one day, a pause:
She hovers a moment, stops uncertainly.
What's this? At the far end of the passage
A new door
A door she's never seen before
Though that's impossible, for
Every nook and cranny in her house
Is known to her.

How did it get here? Where does it lead?
She must go through and see.
She shivers, though it is not cold,
Stares at the door, then turns uneasily away.
Whatever's there will have to wait,
She'll sort it out another, later day.

Sleep

Where do you go to when you're fast asleep?
It's strange. I lie so close to you
I hear your every breath, and yet
You are not with me. You're alone,
Wandering in some far-off land unknown.
It's dark. Who knows what dangers lurk?
You're lost. You call to me.
But here's the rub: I cannot reach you, cannot leap
The hundred year-old hedge, so prickly steep.
So, nightly we abandon one another
To the deep, impenetrable mysteries
Of sleep.

The Perfectionist

Success was often just within his grasp
But then he let it go –
He let it pass:
The thing was not quite perfect yet,
Not absolutely right.
Oh, he could tell –
There was a colour or a shape, a smell
That he must capture, trap, pin down,
And then, and only then, he'd go to town.
But this, the final clinch, the holy grail
Eluded him.
Year after year we saw him fail
In sight of Eldorado
Til he grew quite frail
And all his wit and talent
That promised wonders
Was to no avail.

Last Rose

(For my sister)

We thought she'd slipped away that night,
So small, so frail, so seeming slight.
But no.
Next morning she sat up
And saw the late October light.
'Oh, look', she said.
'We've got another sunny day.'

And then you brought her a red rose,
Large, fully open, with a scent
Richer than all remembered summers spent
With us as children.

'Aaah', she breathed,
Dipping her tiny face
Into the wanton bosom of the flower,
Eyes shut, inhaling.
A long draw, tender 'aaah'.
Delight.

We smell it with her.
She can touch, taste smell.
She can see and hear.
Senses still working.
Can it be true the end is near?

A three-and-a-half pound baby born before
The incubator era
She learned how to fight:
This day and all succeeding days
Are hers by right.

So she's alive
Alive still to delight
The scent of every moment
Yet aware
It fades so quietly, so fast,
Too fast,
This melancholy
Late
October light.

Under the Spell

I can't get you out of my mind
Your skin on mine
The way our limbs so simply
Intertwine
Of their own will
And all my secrets open up to you
As if they knew the nature of this spell:
No ill
Can come to those who love so well
And are so true.

Limbo

We keep in touch with her by Skype, the brother said.
We see a blank, white face.
The eyes are dead
The mouth a scarlet lipstick gash,
The smile a rivet. Fixed.
Where are you, Irene?
She utters not a word.
Who would have thought we'd miss
The sardonic glint, the cruel quip
That wounded more than it amused?
The silent image hovers.
Are you alive or dead
Or in some dreaded limbo in between?
Wouldn't you like to know? she would have said,
Taunting, as in some ancient childhood fight.
Perhaps, when the mind dies
The body stays suspended
Between life and death
With nothing to sustain it
But it's breath.
Enough.
Irene, good ni–i–ight. Irene, goodnight.
Goodnight Irene, good night, Irene,
We'll see you in our dreams.

To W.S. on his 400ᵗʰ Death Day

What does it matter if you lost your head
To gravediggers, long after you were dead?
Or that the bed you left your wife was not your best?
You hugged your secrets tightly to your chest
But left us all a looking glass so clear
We learned to see ourselves in it.
Each hope and fear, each flaw and virtue,
All we hold most dear, reflected in your gaze,
Our jokes, our tantrums, the little ways
That make us human, all there in the plays.
Why look for them in any other place?
To read and watch and listen is to face
Ourselves − and be amazed:
Your passion and your truth still light our days.

The Player

Drama was always much more real to you
Than your own life.
The passions and the sufferings on stage
Released in you the love and hope
And bottled rage
So tightly locked inside you.
Now, with age
You're forced to watch the action from the wings,
An oblique view.
It's more than strange.
People and faces blur.
They wave their arms about but cannot stir
Remembrance of the words they sing or shout
And so you can't tell what the play's about.
And all the parts you've played to great applause
Have ended with their curtain calls
And –
      Lights down. –
                  Fade.

Late Blossoming

Late for school, late for work.
You'll be late
For your own wedding, they all said.
And now I am blossoming, at last
In view of the end gate.

It's good to be myself after a past
Of being what they wanted me to be.
The only thing that can upset me now is this:
I'm haunted by the memory of a tree.

It stood there, in that corner, over there:
A cherry which flowered, as cherries do,
Each year. And then, one spring
When it was very old

A miracle

A wonder, covered in foaming flower,
Each petal like the whites of childrens' eyes
Not just wide open, but eagerly opened wide,
Blooming with all its energy and power.

Oh, look at me, I'm a cherry tree, it cried.
And then, as suddenly
It died.

CPSIA information can be obtained
at www.ICGtesting.com
Printed in the USA
JSHW022233060622
26782JS00001B/34

9 781914 228674

LATE
SUNLIGHT